Inspiring Words
FROM THE PSALMS

Presented to

Presented by

Date

Inspiring Words
FROM THE PSALMS
FOR FRIENDS

SPIRIT PRESS

Inspiring Words from the Psalms for Friends
ISBN 1-40372-041-X

Published in 2006 by Spirit Press, an imprint of Dalmatian Press, LLC.
Copyright © 2006 Dalmatian Press, LLC. Franklin, Tennessee 37067.

Compiler and Editor: Lila Empson
Writers: Margaret Langstaff and Phillip H. Barnhart
Text Design: Diane Whisner

06 07 08 09 WAI 10 9 8 7 6 5 4 3 2 1

14927

Sunrise breaks through
the darkness for good people.

PSALM 112:4 THE MESSAGE

Contents

Introduction

Through friends, God pulls up a chair and sits down in your life. From that position, he is close enough to hear what you say and feel what you leave unsaid. He is near enough to hold and hug you when you need a touch of special love. Friends are one of God's ways of taking care of you. They are presents that God enables you to give yourself.

In the book of Psalms, the whole of human life is represented, including friendship. Insight into friendship abounds. Verse after verse demonstrates its strength, guidance, and encouragement. You can learn about friendship in the book of Psalms. You can also learn about the source of friendship in the book of Psalms. It is God, who gives you friends, helps make you a friend, and dwells in your friendships.

Lord, who may enter your Temple? Who may worship on Zion, your sacred hill? Those who obey God in everything and always do what is right, whose words are true and sincere, and who do not slander others. They do no wrong to their friends nor spread rumors about their neighbors.

Psalm 15:1–3 GNT

Friends Support Each Other

I come to you for shelter. Protect me,
keep me safe, and don't disappoint me.

PSALM 25:20 CEV

The phone rings as you are fixing supper. You have five minutes to get the casserole in the oven before you have to pick up the kids from ball practice. "Hi," a familiar voice says. "Can you talk?" You start to explain how hectic things are and ask if you can call back later, but something in that familiar voice isn't quite right. "Sure," you say, glancing at the kitchen clock. "What's up?"

Your friend is at her wit's end. She has no one she can talk to about her problems, no one who cares as much as you. Though you know a single phone conversation can't solve her problem, you also know you can help lift her spirits. Suddenly all of your priorities are rearranged. Nothing is more important at that instant than being there for your friend.

God is your model for friendship. He is never too
busy to hear your cry for help, never too distracted
to reach out to you when you need him.

Give ear, O LORD, to
my prayer; listen to my
cry of supplication. In
the day of my trouble I
call on you, for you
will answer me.

PSALM 86:6–7 NRSV

Friends Are Kind

*I celebrate and shout because you are kind. You saw
all my suffering, and you cared for me.*

PSALM 31:7 CEV

Two women went to lunch at a nice restaurant to celebrate one's recent promotion at work. The one who had received the promotion had struggled with hostile coworkers and a difficult boss. Through this dark period on the job, it seemed that no one appreciated her work. Credit for her accomplishments often went to her boss. During those difficult months, she poured her heart out to her friend, who was always there to listen and to sypmathize.

Now sitting in the restaurant with her loyal and long-suffering friend, she realized what a trial it must have been for her, too. All the whining and complaining must have nearly driven her crazy. embarrassed and full of regret for having been a burden, she started to apologize. "Don't be silly," her friend said, interrupting. "You are like a sister to me."

*The word "kind" is derived from "kin," which
means "relative." You are a sister or brother to
everyone in God's family. Friendship is the
kindness god wants you to show others.*

During danger he will keep me safe in his shelter. He will hide me in his Holy Tent, or he will keep me safe on a high mountain.

PSALM 27:5 NCV

Friends Offer Advice

*You will guide me with Your counsel, and
afterward receive me to glory.*

PSALM 73:24 NKJV

The Lord works on you through the circumstances of your life. He has given you friends for inspiration, advice, and correction in your many steps along life's journey. When you see a friend stumbling or struggling, first pray humbly to God for the wisdom and compassion to reach out and help. Then, with the help of his Spirit, offer honest, heartfelt advice for the situation your friend is facing.

She may be having a problem at work or with her family; she may have an emotional or financial difficulty; it may be that she is experiencing spiritual drought or confusion about what path to take next. Large or small, usual or unusual, problems plague her life because she is human. Allow yourself to be an instrument of peace and love to your friend for the sake of God's love for you.

*Remain open to God's amazing grace, which will
empower you as his instrument to help those who
need help. Allow him to make your heart
responsive and wise in counseling your friends.*

Happy are those who do not follow the advice of the wicked, or take the path that sinners tread, or sit in the seat of scoffers; but their delight is in the law of the LORD, and on his law they meditate day and night.

PSALM 1:1–2 NRSV

Friends Are Faithful

I will not stop loving David or fail to keep my promise to him.

PSALM 89:33 GNT

A circle of friends, women who had grown up together but had drifted apart, decided to hold a reunion. Everyone in the group was turning fifty that year, and someone had decided that meeting in New York City for a weekend of theater, dining, and shopping would be a grand idea.

Elaborate plans were made and mailings were followed by many phone calls. During the planning, bits of news flew back and forth. A few divorces, children graduated from college, career successes and failures, a child lost in a tragic accident, parents' failing health. These were old and dear friends, and they could not wait to be reunited midway through their lives to share memories and news.

At the last minute, one of the women was unable to attend, which disappointed her deeply. The group, however, refused to let her feel forgotten—they called her every day during the weekend to relate each day's events and news.

Always hold fast to God's example of steady, unwavering love for your friends.

In him our hearts rejoice, for we are trusting in his holy name. Let your unfailing love surround us, LORD, for our hope is in you alone.

PSALM 33:21–22 NLT

Friends Share Love

For the sake of my relatives and friends I will say,
"Peace be within you."

PSALM 122:8 NRSV

Friends have a relationship based on trust, understanding, and shared memories. And each friendship is uniquely defined by the two characters and personalities involved. Amy and Louise met in a bookstore in the same aisle looking for titles by the same author. They began talking and realized they had read many of the same books and appreciated many of the same qualities about the author.

After adjourning to the bookstore café for coffee, they discovered that their lives, however, were very different. Amy was a single computer programmer, while Louise was a nurse and mother of three. But something about their shared interest in books kept alive their interest in each other. Their friendship bloomed, and over time they let each other into their own private worlds, encouraging and supporting each other in their everyday lives.

God delivers the people you need and the people
who need you. He grants you the ability to
recognize and rejoice in these people as his gifts.

The LORD watches over the lives of the innocent, and their reward will last forever.

PSALM 37:18 NCV

Friends Sympathize

*Give great joy to those who have stood
with me in my defense.*

PSALM 35:27 NLT

Tina had been laid up in bed for three weeks. Her husband came home from work early each day to look after her and their two children, and each morning he made lunches for the kids and got them off to school. But they missed their mother. The youngest one had become particularly hard to deal with, and Paul didn't know what to do.

One day, Paul's church friend and tennis partner Kenny came by to check on Tina. Returning from the bedroom, he came into the kitchen where Paul stood at the sink and said, "Tina's doing well."

Paul sighed. "Yes, she is."

Kenny picked up on the sigh and said, "But you're not, right?"

Paul put down a dishtowel and turned. There were tears in his eyes. "Let's go out on the porch and talk things over," Kenny said. "I think I know what you're going through."

*A true friend is someone who reaches for your
hand and touches your heart.*

Friendship with God is
reserved for those who
reverence him. With
them alone he shares the
secrets of his promises.

PSALM 25:14 TLB

Friends Understand

*I know the LORD is always with me. I will not be
shaken, for he is right beside me.*

PSALM 16:8 NLT

A middle-aged woman lived across the street from an elderly man who had recently lost his wife after having been married for more than fifty years. He was not in good health, and his grief was deep and abiding. When spring came, the man began caring for his late wife's many perennials and roses. The woman across the street saw him in the yard often, tending and cutting flowers. Many times he told her he was getting a bouquet together to take to the cemetery.

By June, the old gentleman began showing up at her front door with flowers. Usually she was in the middle of something, but she knew she had to stop and spend some time with him. She felt his loneliness and suspected she reminded him of his wife at that age.

*Always try to look into the hearts of your
friends and meet their needs, even as God
knows the deepest needs of your heart and
never fails to provide for them.*

He led me to a place of
safety; he rescued me
because he delights in me.
The LORD rewarded me
for doing right; he
compensated me because
of my innocence.

PSALM 18:19–20 NLT

Friends Forgive

You are my help. Because of your protection, I sing.

PSALM 63:7 NCV

"Oops—I forgot!" Perhaps the most common source of irritation and disappointment between friends has to do with forgetfulness.

Forgotten birthdays, anniversaries, lunch dates, promises to do something. Unfortunately, it's so easy to do and such an ordinary human failing that most people are guilty of this at some time or another.

A safety net protects true friendships, though, for they are sustained by uncondi-tional love and trust that each friend is sin-cere in wanting to do right by the other. Disappointment stings and creates anger, but it passes when friends realize that intentions were good and that only the execution was faulty. One of the great com-forts of having and being a good friend is the knowledge that you are accepting, and accepted—faults and all, just as you are—without having to try to be anyone else.

God will guide you as you try to conform your behavior to his, particularly when you're dealing with forgiveness. Everyone makes mistakes and needs to be forgiving and forgiven.

Gracious is the LORD, and righteous; yes, our God is merciful. The LORD preserves the simple; I was brought low, and He saved me.

PSALM 116:5-6 NKJV

Friends Are Compassionate

Many a time turned he his anger away,
and did not stir up all his wrath.

PSALM 78:38 KJV

here, but for the grace of God, go I." Compassion is standing in the other person's shoes. Compassion is knowing the same thing could happen to you. Compassion is identifying fully with the other person and feeling just as he or she does in trying circumstances as well as in happy times.

God is full of compassion, and he is your example. In every instance that Jesus was moved by the sufferings of others, he acted immediately to alleviate their pain. Being compassionate consistently is not easy. In fact, it hurts. It involves leaving your heart open to all the ups and downs of life that affect others. You become vulnerable, sensitive, and tender. Because the difficulties of others demand a caring response from you, you must become active. You can't just watch from the sidelines; you must reach out and help.

Ask God to remove all self-protective hardness
from your heart and send you the grace necessary
to be compassionate always.

They will be so kind and
merciful and good, that they
will be a light in the dark for
others who do the right thing.

PSALM 112:4 CEV

Friends Stand Fast

I declare that your steadfast love is established
forever; your faithfulness is as firm as the heavens.

PSALM 89:2 NRSV

It's easy to know who your friends are when big trouble hits: job loss, divorce, serious illness, financial reversal, legal problems. Acquaintances don't want much to do with sad or desperate situations. And opportunists don't hang around after you no longer can be of any use to them.

Bill's business went bust years after he had invested all of his time and money in it. When he had to file bankruptcy, his wife left with the kids. He was fifty-nine, and it was hard for him to find a job. One golfing buddy remained loyal, as did his bird dog and his former office cleaning lady, who cleaned the studio apartment he now called home. In this, Bill found a sobering and inspiring lesson about friendship: Friends love you because of who you are, not what you have. He counted himself blessed to have three true friends who had stood the ultimate test.

Pray that you always have the courage to stand by your
friends, and that they, in turn, remain loyal to you.

The LORD is my shepherd;
I shall not want.
He makes me to lie down in green pastures;
He leads me beside the still waters.
He restores my soul;
He leads me in the paths of righteousness
for His name's sake.

PSALM 23:1–3 NKJV

Friends Speak the Truth

*Justice and judgment are the habitation of thy
throne: mercy and truth shall go before thy face.*

PSALM 89:14 KJV

Mary and Lucinda, high-school juniors, went shopping for prom
dresses one afternoon. Though shopping was fun, it was serious
business picking out just the right ensemble for such an important
occasion. The selections were overwhelming
in their variety, and it took them hours to
narrow down the choices.

Lucinda, who was a perfect size seven,
made a choice first. Mary's decision-making
was more complicated, because she was
more full-figured. But finally Mary fell in love with a dress and asked
Lucinda for her approval. Both were tired, and it was late in the day.

Mary modeled a beautiful midnight blue dress. But it was form-
fitting and didn't flatter her figure. "It's not right," Lucinda said,
shaking her head and feeling bad for her friend. "It's too, I don't
know, tight or something. It just doesn't make you look as pretty as
you are."

*No matter how difficult, it is your responsibility to
always offer honest, reliable advice to your friends.*

*G*od's word is true,
and everything he does is right.
He loves what is right and fair;
the LORD's love fills the earth.

PSALM 33:4–5 NCV

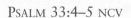

Friends Are Gentle

*Light shines in the darkness for good people, for
those who are merciful, kind and just.*

PSALM 112:4 GNT

The Walkers and the Bennetts were weekly tennis doubles part-
ners and had been for more than five years. They had played in a

couple of club tournaments together—Bob
and Mike pairing off, Betty and Jane team-
ing up—against other opponents. Their
friendship as couples had blossomed and
matured over time.

In the last year Bob Walker's career had
stalled, and he was having trouble with his
boss. Sometimes he would come to their
tennis games dragging and down in the mouth. Betty tried to make
up for his gloom by being cheerful and outgoing. The Bennetts made
an extra effort not to push Bob too hard in the match until he had
time to loosen up and forget his troubles. Their understanding of the
delicate situation and their patience with Bob's moods helped the
Walkers through a difficult time.

*If you take the time to be gentle with your friends'
feelings, God will help you to offer the right
comfort and encouragement at the right time.*

I will sing each morning about your power and mercy. For you have been my high tower of refuge, a place of safety in the day of my distress. O my Strength, to you I sing my praises; for you are my high tower of safety, my God of mercy.

PSALM 59:16–17 TLB

Friends Are Long-Suffering

His heart is fixed, trusting in the LORD.

PSALM 112:7 KJV

Five women had worked together at a publishing company in New York—their first jobs out of college. As young singles, they became fast friends and did everything together. But when their paths

and careers diverged, they made a commitment to stay involved in one another's lives.

As time passed, most married and had children, some left work, most continued in some facet of business. Yet their ties only deepened with each new milestone marked in life. When they reached middle age, one of them fell seriously ill, and the prognosis was very bad. The extended chronic illness challenged the women in ways they could not have imagined. They were called to minister to their friend and help each other in handling the sorrow to such a degree that they were strained often to the breaking point.

When your heart is fixed on God, you become a
window of his constant love to those around you.
He gives you an intuitive sense of right behavior
with respect to your friends.

You who live in the shelter of the Most High,
who abide in the shadow of the Almighty, will
say to the LORD, "My refuge and my fortress;
my God, in whom I trust."

PSALM 91:1–2 NRSV

Friends Protect Each Other

I have respected your laws, so keep me safe.

PSALM 119:94 CEV

You may have memories of the schoolyard bully and the friends who stood by to protect you when he threatened to attack. As you grow older, your friends' protection becomes more subtle and complex.

Sarah and Katherine became friends after seeing each other in the park with their young children a couple of times a week. While the kids played, they exchanged life histories, wishes, hopes, and dreams. While Sarah had a stable, happy marriage, she often picked up clues in conversation that Katherine's home life was less than perfect. One day, a downcast Katherine came to the park with her eyes red and swollen, as if from crying. She offered no explanation for her appearance.

"If you ever need me," Sarah said as they parted that day, "call me, no matter what time it is, okay? I mean it." Sarah squeezed Katherine's shoulder.

"I will," Katherine said. "I will."

As God protects you with his unbounded love, so you are responsible for safeguarding your friends.

Satisfy us in the morning
with your steadfast love,
so that we may rejoice
and be glad all our days.

PSALM 90:14 NRSV

Friends Share All

Pour out your unfailing love on those who know you!

PSALM 36:10 TLB

The most valuable commodity you have today is time. Unlike goods and services, extra time in your daily life is probably in short supply. And friendship requires an investment of time, above all else. But opportunities exist everywhere for integrating friendships into the overall fabric of your daily life. Indeed, including your friends in the mundane of everyday living can draw you nearer and create familylike ties among all of you. Friends need to participate in each other's lives, not simply get together for special occasions. Just hanging out together—doing things around the house, helping with difficult tasks, or mulling things over—builds intimacy and security among friends. This in turn is relied upon when emergencies or tough times arise, for you know almost intuitively what to do for your friends.

With God's help, you can develop the generosity of spirit to fully become a part of your friends' lives. Then you can give to them in the fullness of your heart, as God gives of himself to you.

I will thank you, LORD,
with all my heart;
I will tell of all the
marvelous things
you have done.
I will be filled with
joy because of you.
I will sing praises to your
name, O Most High.

PSALM 9:1–2 NLT

Friends Enjoy Each Other's Company

*Light shines on the godly, and joy
on those who do right.*

PSALM 97:11 NLT

The doorbell rang Sunday afternoon as Marty was folding laundry. Monday was already on her mind, with all the strain of getting the kids to school and herself to the office on time. The work left on her desk Friday afternoon was beginning to haunt her. How could she get it all done? When she opened the door, her mood softened and brightened. It was Theresa, her friend from down the street.

"You've got to come over and see what I've done with that room!" she cried. "You won't recognize it!" Theresa's face was all smiles.

Marty looked over her shoulder toward the laundry room and the Monday morning gaining on her and made her decision. She knew Theresa had been pondering for weeks what color to paint the spare bedroom. Marty couldn't wait to share in her pleasure and surprise.

*The visitation of a good friend is like a breath from
heaven. Her companionship is a blessing from God
that bolsters and comforts you.*

*J*oin me in giving glory
to the LORD. Let us
honor him together.

PSALM 34:3 NIrV

Friends Work Side by Side

The godly people in the land are my true heroes!
I take pleasure in them!

PSALM 16:3 NLT

The renowned musician was giving a brilliant organ concert in a famous old church. At the top of his skills, he had left the audience breathless. No one had ever heard anything like it.

Intermission came, and the musician climbed down from the organ bench to take a well-deserved rest. He walked around behind the organ where he saw Robert, his friend of many years, sitting on a chair by the place where air was pumped into the organ so it could be played. His friend was the one who did the pumping. Robert smiled at the great musician and said, "We're giving them quite a concert, aren't we?"

The musician returned the smile and said, "You know I couldn't do it without you."

It is a great development in your life when you
come to realize that you and your friends can do a
better job on something together than any of you
can do alone. God blesses those who work together
in love and with joy.

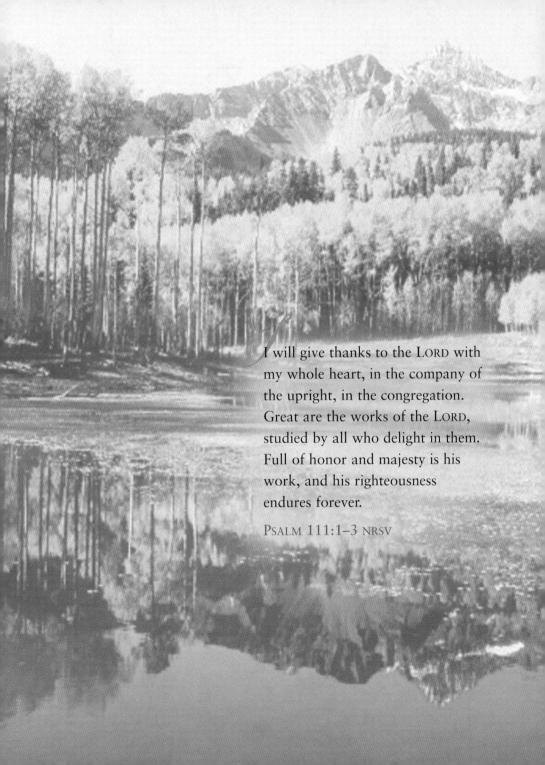

I will give thanks to the LORD with
my whole heart, in the company of
the upright, in the congregation.
Great are the works of the LORD,
studied by all who delight in them.
Full of honor and majesty is his
work, and his righteousness
endures forever.

PSALM 111:1–3 NRSV

Friends Make Sacrifices

*He has delivered me from every trouble, and my
eye has looked in triumph on my enemies.*

PSALM 54:7 NRSV

Jerry and Janet hadn't had a weekend to themselves in months. Jerry had been traveling on business, and Janet, a medical doctor, had been on weekend rotations in the emergency room. They longed for quiet time alone together at home.

Friday night, as they were sitting in front of the TV with their arms linked, they received a frantic phone call. It was Barb; she and Allen were moving that weekend.

"I hate to ask this," Barb said, her voice full of regret, "but we've had a problem with the movers."

Janet looked across the room at her weary husband. "And you need help, right?" she asked. She put her hand over the receiver and explained to Jerry. They'd had their own difficulties with moving.

"Let's do it," Jerry said finally.

"You bet," Janet replied.

*The demands that love places upon the heart are
rarely convenient or moderate. But as God is
always there for you, you must be available to your
friends when they need you.*

Accept my prayer as incense offered to you, and my upraised hands as an evening offering.

PSALM 141:2 NLT

Friends Pray Together

In the day when I cried out, You answered me,
and made me bold with strength in my soul.

PSALM 138:3 NKJV

Joan, Allie, and Betsy have an active and fruitful prayer group. Every week they exchange prayer requests and spend a half-hour a day praying for the items on the list. Their prayer requests are specific and timely, relating to what is really going on in their lives. They also include big requests, such as world peace, the salvation of souls, and a solution to world hunger.

They have prayed like this for years, ever since Allie's father fell seriously ill and was in intensive care. During his illness they met over the phone three times a day in a conference call, asking God to make him well. Allie's father recovered, and the three friends developed a deepened spirituality and prayer life. Their prayers have continued to be answered, and they give credit to God for the security, joy, and abundance they have found in their lives.

Pray that your friends, and everyone's friends,
discover the joy and comfort of praying for and
with each other.

You, O Lord, are a God merciful and gracious, slow to anger and abounding in steadfast love and faithfulness.

PSALM 86:15 NRSV

Friends Receive Special Blessings from God

*My life is an example to many, because you have
been my strength and protection.*

PSALM 71:7 NLT

Friendship develops and grows and prospers over time. It requires
space and grace. Like a huge tree, it needs to root deeply and spread
its branches. With each obstacle overcome, each
crisis survived, and many ordinary days in
between, it becomes stronger and more valuable, in exactly the same way that your relationship with God deepens and flourishes as
you repeatedly seek his company and help.

God works through his people. He sends
friends to give you aid and comfort. When you
recognize this and give thanks and stick with your friends, abundant
blessings flow to you, both individually and in the friendship relationship. God honors friendships with special blessings and strength.
The lives of your friends reflect the confidence and grace that God
bestows, and they become shining examples to others.

*Allow God to guide you and teach you to be a
loyal and giving friend so that you may be an
instrument of his glory and grace in the world.*

The LORD will give strength to His people;
the LORD will bless His people with peace.

PSALM 29:11 NKJV

Friends Are United

*He will redeem me unharmed from the battle that I
wage, for many are arrayed against me.*

PSALM 55:18 NRSV

Gail and Linda were neighbors who both had teenage daughters
attending the same high school. The girls were good friends and did
just about everything together. Gail's daughter, Susie, was an extro-
vert and always full of energy; while Linda's
daughter, Marie, was relatively shy and
reserved. They tempered each other's excesses
and had complementary traits.

One evening Marie went to her mother
with troubling news. Someone had been
spreading reputation-wrecking rumors around
school about Susie's behavior with boys and
drugs. Marie knew these stories were untrue,
but she feared for Susie, who was terribly upset about them. All four
of the friends—both mothers and both daughters—went to see the
guidance counselor at school the next day. They confronted the problem as a group and received immediate results from the school
authorities, thus ending the spread of all damaging rumors.

*God watches over your friends and protects them;
he gives you the courage to stand by them when
they need you and the wisdom to do what is right.*

I have set the LORD always before me: because he is at my right hand, I shall not be moved. Therefore my heart is glad, and my glory rejoiceth: my flesh also shall rest in hope.

PSALM 16:8–9 KJV

Friends Are Generous

*You give your guests a feast in your house, and you
serve a tasty drink that flows like a river.*

PSALM 36:8 CEV

Three sorority sisters shared everything from hair dryers and
clothes to food, money, cars, and textbooks. When they graduated,

they kept in touch and got together
each summer at a beach cottage.
There, they spent a week in the sun
catching up on the year's news, reading, reminiscing, and laying out plans
for the great things they were going
to do in life. Always they exchanged
information, contacts, and advice—anything one had that another
needed.

It was a special time in the year to which they always looked forward—reuniting with best friends and giving of themselves to main-
tain the friendship. In fact, the three women, now middle-aged with
grown children, still continue the tradition. The time spent together
is one of the big highlights of their year and an important factor in
their lives.

*God can teach you to extend yourself for your
friends and to give to them abundantly. Through
God's abundant generosity, you learn the joy of
giving and the blessings derived from it.*

*A*re there those who respect the LORD? He will point them to the best way. They will enjoy a good life, and their children will inherit the land. The LORD tells his secrets to those who respect him; he tells them about his agreement. My eyes are always looking to the LORD for help. He will keep me from any traps.

PSALM 25:12–15 NCV

Friends Bring Out the Best in Each Other

*Delight thyself also in the LORD; and he shall give
thee the desires of thine heart.*

PSALM 37:4 KJV

There are many tests of friendship. But perhaps the ultimate test lies in how effective the relationship is in bringing each friend closer to God. Worldly achievements and success usually attach themselves to believers; however, that is not the point of one's life. The "best" that you can be truly means to completely conform your life to God and, thereby, find true happiness and peace.

Make deepened spirituality the measure of the quality of your friendships. Are you encouraging spiritual growth, prayer, moral and ethical development, and participation in a community of believers? Do you avoid putting your friends in the way of temptation? Do you forbear from contributing to behavior that is dangerous to the health of their souls? Do you offer consistent, selfless encouragement and advice directed to the well-being and growth of your friends' spiritual lives?

*Strive to achieve the grace necessary to bring out
the best in your friends and to do all you can to
bring them ever closer to God.*

The godly shall be firmly
planted in the land, and
live there forever. The
godly man is a good
counselor because he is
just and fair and knows
right from wrong.

PSALM 37:29–31 TLB

Friends Inspire Each Other

Bless the LORD, O my soul.

PSALM 104:1 KJV

"Look at you! Look at what you've done!" Heidi yelled across the fairway. Her golfing partner, Linda, had effortlessly birdied the first hole; this, after confessing to Heidi before they teed off that she was convinced her golf game was getting worse instead of better. She was even thinking of giving it up altogether. This statement had really concerned Heidi, because their weekly game was the only regular time they were able to spend together.

"That's a really tough hole, kiddo," Heidi said as Linda putted out two over par. "I'm proud of you. Look how you can play when you stop trying so hard!"

Linda smiled ruefully. "Maybe I've turned the corner," she said. Linda thought, *Heidi never stops encouraging me, never teases me too hard when I flub a shot. I really enjoy being with her.*

When you search for the right words and tone of voice, you can be a source of hope and inspiration to your friends in matters both great and small.

You have turned for me my mourning into dancing; You have put off my sackcloth and clothed me with gladness, to the end that my glory may sing praise to You and not be silent. O LORD my God, I will give thanks to You forever.

PSALM 30:11–12 NKJV

Friends Encourage Each Other

Everyone finds shelter in the
shadow of your wings.

PSALM 36:7 CEV

Karen had always wanted to be an artist. More than anything else, she loved to paint and draw. But financial constraints kept her from pursuing her dream with all of her time and energy. To contribute to the family income, she worked as an x-ray technician at a local hospital. On weekends, though, she pursued her artwork. Finally, after years, she had enough work to take to an art show.

Her friend Deborah, a nurse, had watched and nurtured Karen's artistic pursuits—always asking about what she was working on, analyzing it, and praising it. Deborah knew the importance of following one's dreams and making use of one's God-given talents. Deborah pitched in when the time came for Karen to go to the art show. Deborah helped Karen set up and stayed with her. Deborah's encouragement to Karen was immeasurable.

You can look into the hearts of your friends, discern
what makes them who they are, and nurture their
uniqueness so they can flower as God intends.

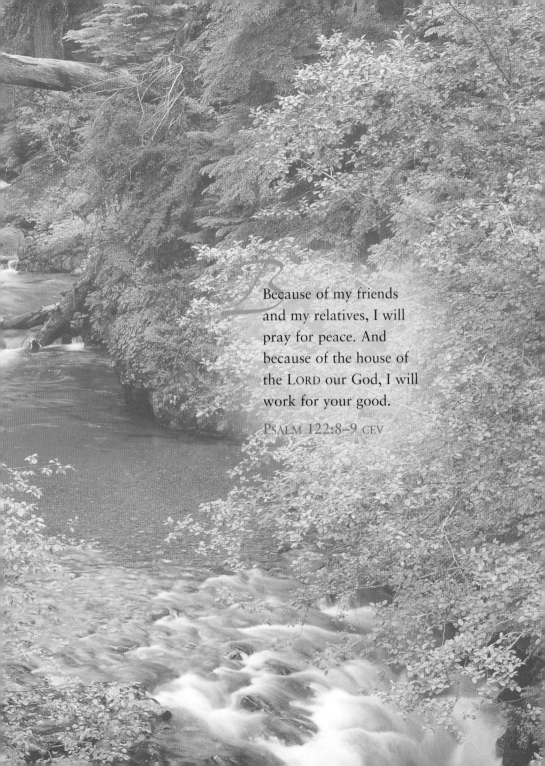

Because of my friends
and my relatives, I will
pray for peace. And
because of the house of
the LORD our God, I will
work for your good.

PSALM 122:8–9 CEV

Friends Dream Together

Let heaven and earth praise Him, the seas
and everything that moves in them.

PSALM 69:34 NKJV

Carpooling to and from work gave Sara, Lynn, and Jeanie plenty of time over the year to get to know one another. Creeping along in rush-hour traffic, they developed a friendship and knowledge of one another's family and interests. Sara hoped her young son would continue with his piano lessons and practice, because he showed signs of being a child prodigy. Lynn and her husband were planning their dream home and hoped to begin construction within a year. Jeanie wanted to finish her college degree and hoped to find the time and money to do just that.

The more they opened up to one another, the more their friendship grew. They each came to share their aspirations, until they truly had invested themselves in the others' dreams. They began to pray for one another that these dreams would become a reality; and as they did, their confidence grew and real progress was made.

An important part of friendship is becoming open
enough to participate in the dreams of others.

Be still in the presence of
the LORD, and wait
patiently for him to act.

PSALM 37:7 NLT

God Blesses the Bonds of Friendship

The mouths of the righteous utter wisdom,
and their tongues speak justice.

PSALM 37:30 NRSV

Two women who had been friends for years decided to open a catering business together. They had given the idea and their business  plan a great deal of thought and had reviewed it with accountants and outside advisers. Both women were hard workers, creative and energetic, and they were aware of the tough path they were choosing. They were knowledgeable about the difficulties and obstacles they would encounter at start-up. They prayerfully sought guidance from God in their decision, as well as help from him in building the business.

The things that really set the new business apart from other wannabes were the pair's knowledge, understanding, and confidence in each other. They had been through tough times together before. They knew each other well, and they trusted each other and God implicitly. They made a winning team.

When you seek God's guidance with your
friendships, he will never let you down, but will
strengthen and bless them abundantly.

Commit everything you do to the LORD. Trust him, and he will help you. He will make your innocence as clear as the dawn, and the justice of your cause will shine like the noonday sun.

PSALM 37:5–6 NLT

Friends Rest in Each Other's Strength

Good people suffer many troubles, but the
LORD saves them from them all.

PSALM 34:19 GNT

Christina was having one of those days. Everything was running about an hour late: her dentist appointment, her trip to the grocery store. The traffic was awful. Then, as she was speeding along the interstate en route to Happy Camper Childcare to pick up little Travis, she heard a horrible bang! Her car lurched to the right, nearly careening over the shoulder of the roadbed into a ditch. When it finally came to a stop and she had stopped shaking, she realized she'd had a blowout.

The ice cream was melting, the chicken was defrosting, the Novocain was wearing off, her jaw hurt, and, worst of all, Happy Camper Childcare would close in fifteen minutes and Travis would be out on the street. She fumbled for her cell phone. "Lisa?" she gasped when her friend answered. "Thank God you're home! I really need your help."

Friends are God's angels sent to keep you safe. Praise
God and thank him for the wonderful gift of friendship.

Our LORD and our God,
you are like the sun and
also like a shield. You
treat us with kindness
and with honor, never
denying any good thing
to those who live right.

PSALM 84:11 CEV

Friends Correct Each Other

I will advise you and watch your progress.

PSALM 32:8 TLB

Martha listened and felt her heart sinking as Abby's voice rose with enthusiasm. Abby was describing the dining room suite she had run across at a furniture store. It was just what she had been looking for, and, best of all, it was on sale. "And you know better than anyone, Martha," Abby said, "how long I've been trying to find a Southwest style around here where there are nothing but nineteenth-century repro- ductions."

"But I thought you'd made it a priority to pay off your credit cards, Abby," Martha said. She tensed, knowing that wasn't what Abby wanted to hear. But Martha felt she had to say it. Just last week Abby had said that she was getting in over her head and needed to curb her spending.

God can use you to guide and correct your friends as needed. If you are attentive to him, he will put the right words in your mouth and the right spirit in your heart so that you may do this gently.

God is our refuge and strength,
a very present help in trouble.

PSALM 46:1 NKJV

Friends Look Out for Each Other

*The eyes of the Lord are intently watching
all who live good lives.*

PSALM 34:15 TLB

Stephanie had been thinking about it all Saturday morning and finally picked up the phone to call Bets, who answered after three rings. "You've been on my mind all morning, Bets. I even had a dream about you last night," Stephanie said.

Bets laughed. "That's funny," she said. "I've been down in the dumps the last couple of days. I'm having trouble at work again."

Stephanie had a sudden inspiration. "Let's go over the classified ads together this Sunday, Bets. I'm sure if we put our heads together, we could come up with some alternatives for you." Bets groaned.

"No, it'll be fun! You've got to start somewhere," Stephanie said.

"You're right, Stephanie. Thanks for pushing me to get going on it."

*When you care deeply for your friends, you become
attuned to their well-being, and many times God
enables you to know intuitively when something is
wrong. You become an extension of God's love and
grace for them in the world.*

$\mathcal{L}$ord, when doubts fill
my mind, when my heart
is in turmoil, quiet me
and give me renewed
hope and cheer.

PSALM 94:19 TLB

Friends Do Not Cause Each Other to Stumble

Show me Your ways, O LORD;
teach me your paths.

PSALM 25:4 NKJV

Katie's doctor laid down the law: Her blood pressure and cholesterol were dangerously high, and she had to lose thirty pounds. He gave her a diet to follow and set her up for weekly weigh-ins. Cora had been worried about Katie's health and was glad that someone had finally gotten through to her, but she knew the diet was not going to be easy for Katie. Katie had a terrible sweet tooth, and when stressed or unhappy she would automatically reach for the candy and milk shakes.

Cora realized she was going to have to change her own behavior around Katie to help her. No more stops at the ice-cream parlor on the way to the mall. No more brownies or strawberry shortcake for dessert. She would have to provide lots of comfort and support for Katie at every appropriate opportunity.

Sacrifice is often required of friends for the good of the other. And it is particularly important to support your friends in their battles against human weaknesses.

I will try to walk a blameless path, but how I need your help, especially in my own home, where I long to act as I should.

PSALM 101:2 TLB

Friends Steady Each Other

Yes, Lord, let your constant love surround us,
for our hopes are in you alone.

PSALM 33:22 TLB

Emily was terrified to give her presentation at work. Her friend Cherise knew all about fears and tried to think of things that would alleviate Emily's nervousness. Emily knew her material and was ready for any questions the audience might have. It wasn't a matter of preparation; it was a matter of confidence.

Cherise suggested they ask God to take care of Emily's presentation delivery. They prayed together over the phone every night for a week, asking specifically for help with the questions. Emily really believed God would intervene, but she wasn't sure she could hold up her end of the bargain. Then, the morning before her speech, Cherise gave her something to hang on to during the presentation. When Emily was called to the podium, she went with her papers in one hand and a small cross in the other. She was dazzling.

You can give your concerns about your friends
to God, and ask him to help you reach out in
the best way when they need you.

The LORD also will be a refuge for the oppressed, a refuge in times of trouble. And those who know Your name will put their trust in You; for You, LORD, have not forsaken those who seek You.

PSALM 9:9–10 NKJV

Friends Celebrate Each Other's Victories

They will abide in prosperity, and their
children shall possess the land.

PSALM 25:13 NRSV

"Way to go, Tim!" A chorus of shouts rang out as he walked tall across the stage of the community college. At forty-three, he had graduated with a degree in computer science. Tim had worked with

computers for years but hadn't had the academic background to advance in his company. Now they would not be able to keep him back. Fourteen of his neighbors resumed their cheering, "That's our Tim!" Tim turned toward the balcony and gave them a thumbs-up.

This neighborhood cheerleading team had begun years before when Tim's next-door neighbor saw that Tim had painted himself into a corner at his job. "Tim," he said one day after a summer block party, "why don't you go back to college and get your degree?" Tim offered the usual reasons, but his friend encouraged him and said, "Tim, everyone in the neighborhood knows you can do it."

The high spots of life often come when friends
encourage your efforts and celebrate your victories.

May He send you help
from the sanctuary and
support you from Zion!

PSALM 20:2 NASB

Friends Bear Each Other Up

The LORD is the strength of my life;
of whom shall I be afraid?
PSALM 27:1 NKJV

There is a story of an old man who carried a little can of oil with him wherever he went. If he passed through a door that squeaked, he poured some oil on the hinges. If a gate was hard to open, he oiled the latch. Once he was seen oiling the back door of a taxicab.

This man went through life lubricating hard places and making it easier for those who came after him. People called him eccentric and other things, but he went steadily on, refilling his can of oil when it became empty and oiling the hard places he found.

You will always be happier when you serve others, when you choose to lift and not to lean. Do something each day that you don't get paid to do. Extend your hand to somebody and extend yourself. Remember that when you help someone up a hill, you get closer to the top yourself. There is nothing more wonderful in life than helping somebody.

The LORD says, "I will rescue those who love me.
I will protect those who trust in my name.
When they call on me, I will answer;
I will be with them in trouble.
I will rescue them and honor them.
I will satisfy them with a long life
and give them my salvation."

PSALM 91–14-16 NLT

Friends Are Reliable

Who is as mighty as you, O LORD?
Your faithfulness surrounds you.

PSALM 89:8 NRSV

Charles Plumb was a United States Navy jet pilot in Vietnam. After seventy-five combat missions, his plane was destroyed by a surface-to-air missile. Plumb ejected and parachuted into enemy hands,

was captured, and spent six years in an enemy prison camp. He survived the ordeal and tells his story wherever he can.

One day, when Plumb and his wife were sitting in a restaurant, a man at another table came up and exclaimed, "You're Plumb! You flew jet fighters from the *Kitty Hawk*! You were shot down!"

Plumb was taken aback by the recognition and sought an explanation. "How in the world did you know that?"

The man proudly replied, "I packed your parachute every day." Plumb got to his feet and energetically shook the man's hand. "Thank you," he said. "I'm here today because of you. Thank you for being someone I could count on."

Everyone has somebody who provides what they need to make it through the day. You pack parachutes for others all the time.

The LORD is a refuge for the oppressed, a place of safety in times of trouble.

PSALM 9:9 GNT

Friends Provide Reality Checks

You are my rock and my fortress; therefore, for Your
name's sake, lead me and guide me.

PSALM 31:3 NKJV

Randy was the youngest partner in a big-city law firm. He specialized in corporate contracts and was exceptionally good at what he did. Randy had one of the best law practices around. Randy also had

a family who needed some of the time his law practice got. He was often gone in the morning before the children got up and out entertaining a client when they went to bed. And his wife felt increasingly neglected.

In addition to his law practice and family, Randy had a friend who would not stand by and watch Randy lose what was more important to him than he seemed to realize. Warren stopped Randy one morning just before he got into his car and insisted they have a talk right then. Randy resisted, but Warren would have it no other way. He would tell his friend the truth.

You can help someone face reality. You can tell
them they need not fear a collision with reality
because that is where God always is.

They will be so kind and merciful and good, that they will be a light in the dark for others who do the right thing. Life will go well for those who freely lend and are honest in business. They won't ever be troubled, and the kind things they do will never be forgotten.

PSALM 112:4–6 CEV

Friends Endure Through Time

You have been with me from birth;
from my mother's womb you have cared for me.

PSALM 71:6 NLT

*O*ld friend is a phrase that evokes warmth and comfort, and for good reason. Your best friends, your most solid and beloved friends, are those who have stood the test of time. They have forgiven your oversights, silliness, every kind of foolishness, petty offenses, and large mistakes. They have seen you at your best as well as your worst. They know your strengths and your weaknesses.

Old friends share memories that nothing can take away. They communicate well because they know each other well. Getting along is not an issue. Instead, the company of friends is a source of quiet joy. Friends can happily spend an afternoon together without saying a word. They have weathered and overcome the ups and downs of life. Friends flourish in the light they create for each other, and they may call themselves blessed.

Pray that you receive the grace for friendship that
endures, for it is one of God's greatest gifts and a
gift that will bring you closer to him.

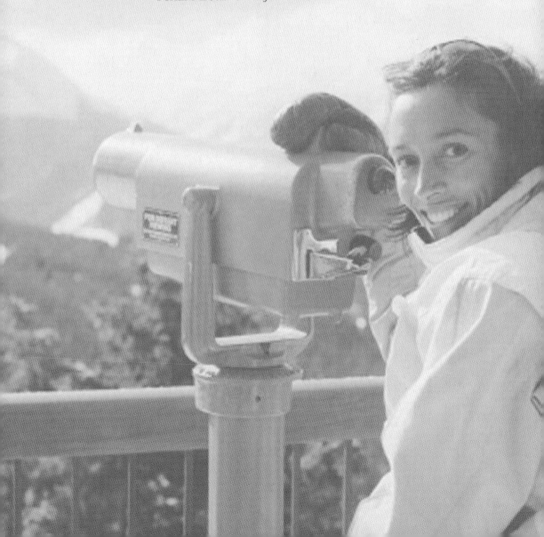

Examine me, O Lord, and prove me;
try my mind and my heart.
For Your lovingkindness is before my eyes,
and I have walked in Your truth.

Psalm 26:2–3 nkjv

Friends Are Accepting

His anger is but for a moment,
His favor is for life.

PSALM 30:5 NKJV

Amy was one of those people who tried to cram as much activity into any given hour in the day as was humanly possible. The result: She was always twenty or thirty minutes late, sometimes more. Sharon and Amy had been friends for years, but Amy's habitual tardiness almost nipped the friendship in the bud. For Sharon, promptness was a matter of honor and principle. Being late was irresponsible and inconsiderate.

Finally, after Amy missed a plane and was fired from a job because of her tardiness, Sharon realized Amy had a problem. Sharon softened and wanted to help. And try to help she did, but with only modest improvement on Amy's part. Sharon at last conceded that being late was just part of being Amy. She resolved to love her just the way she was.

No one is perfect. Accepting and forgiving your friends'
faults is one of the demands of friendship, just as God
accepts and forgives you for your own shortcomings.

You are kind, LORD, so good and merciful. You protect ordinary people, and when I was helpless, you saved me and treated me so kindly that I don't need to worry anymore.

PSALM 116:5–7 CEV

Friends Provide Hugs

The LORD is close to the brokenhearted,
and he saves those whose spirits have been crushed.

PSALM 34:18 NCV

Y ou look like you need a hug," Nancy said as her friend walked into the room. "What's the matter?"

"I don't know. I just don't have much energy," Nita said. Her shoulders slumped a little.

Nancy put her arm around her. "Are you getting enough sleep, kiddo?"

Tears sprang to Nita's eyes. "I'm not getting enough of anything!" she whispered under her breath.

"You've been working too hard, and with the kids and all, it's just too much. You need a little break." Nancy squeezed her shoulder.

Tears ran down Nita's cheeks. "I looked at the trash stacked up in the garage, and it was the last straw. Those big, plastic bags . . ." She covered her face.

"I've got an idea," Nancy said. "You and Ted take the weekend off; do something fun. Let me take care of the kids and clean your house. It's just what you need."

Friends serve and minister to one another's needs,
generously and selflessly, in matters great and small.

$\mathcal{Y}$ou, LORD, have saved my life
from death, my eyes from
tears, my feet from stumbling.
Now I will walk at your side
in this land of the living. I was
faithful to you when I was
suffering, though in my
confusion I said, "I can't
trust anyone!"

PSALM 116:8–11 CEV

Friends Are There When the World Abandons You

I asked the LORD for help, and he answered me.
He saved me from all that I feared.

PSALM 34:4 NCV

Amanda's life had been in a downward spiral for some time. Her increasingly erratic and rash behavior had resulted in bounced checks, heavy debts, and speeding tickets. And the loss of her driver's license had put her teaching job on the line. Her condo was a mess, and the plumbing in one bathroom was backed up.

Most people thought irresponsible willfulness on Amanda's part was to blame. Everyone, that is, except her old college friend Ruth. Ruth remembered the old Amanda and convinced her to see a doctor to talk over all the bad things that had been happening. The doctor discovered that a sizable brain tumor was causing her strange behavior, and immediately scheduled surgery. The operation was successful and, over a period of time, Amanda regained her health and was able to rebuild her life.

Very simply, God will never forsake you, and you
must never forsake your friends. The love of
friendship, as an extension of God's love for the
world, is unconditional and unchanging.

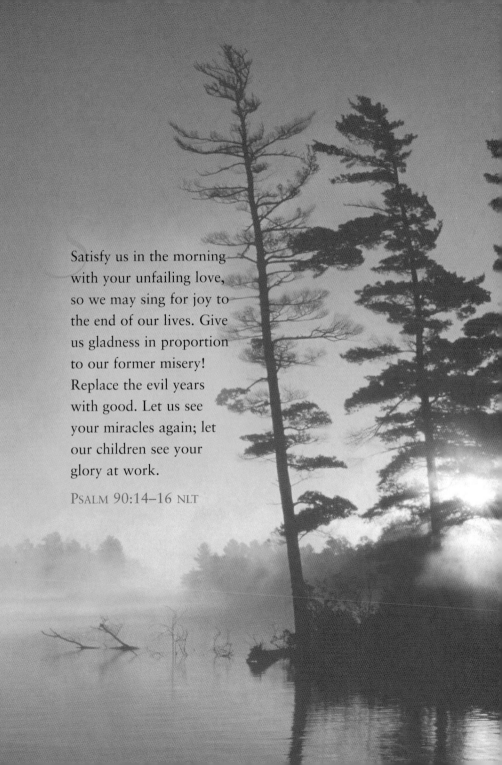

Satisfy us in the morning
with your unfailing love,
so we may sing for joy to
the end of our lives. Give
us gladness in proportion
to our former misery!
Replace the evil years
with good. Let us see
your miracles again; let
our children see your
glory at work.

PSALM 90:14–16 NLT

Friends Minister to Each Other's Wounds

Depend on the LORD; *trust him, and he will take care of you.*

PSALM 37:5 NCV

*I*nvitations had gone out, the church had been reserved, and the bridesmaids had ordered their dresses. Lauren, who was slated to be

a June bride, was crushed when her fiancé backed out of the engagement in the middle of May. Lauren was numb with embarrassment. Nothing in her fiancé's previous behavior had given any clue that something like this might happen.

All her plans for the future had imploded. Ivy, who was to have been her maid of honor, suggested they take a trip together, using the time Lauren had set aside for the honeymoon. Ivy would take an emergency leave from work, and they would drive west across the country, to the Grand Canyon, Colorado, and California. As the miles passed, Lauren would decompress and heal in the company of her good friend. Maybe they would even start laying plans for a new, improved future for Lauren.

When bad things happen to your friends, step up without hesitation, as God does for you, and soothe and support them.

Steadfast love and faithfulness will meet;
righteousness and peace will kiss each other.
Faithfulness will spring up from the ground,
and righteousness will look down from the sky.

PSALM 85:10–11 NRSV

Friends Can Keep Secrets

Trust the LORD and do good.
Live in the land and feed on truth.

PSALM 37:3 NCV

Keeping a secret can be difficult. Secrets come in many flavors and varieties. Happy surprises, great news, shameful or sad, silly and

funny . . . A secret's information must be contained until the proper time comes for disclosure. And for some secrets, that could mean the Second Coming.

There's a maxim that says if you want to keep a secret, keep it to yourself. But sometimes you just have to confide in someone to relieve stress and regain peace of mind. Sometimes, revealing a secret to a trusted friend, and receiving the benefit of his or her counsel, is just plain necessary. When friends share with you in confidence important parts of their lives that they do not want anyone but you to know, you must honor their confidence. Close friends have few secrets from each other. They are able to share almost everything in confidence, because they are able to trust.

God can make you trustworthy to fully share in
your friends' lives and support them.

O LORD, you have
searched me and you
know me. You know
when I sit and when I
rise; you perceive my
thoughts from afar. You
discern my going out and
my lying down; you are
familiar with all my ways.
Before a word is on my
tongue, you know it
completely, O LORD.

PSALM 139:1–4 NIV

Friends Intercede with God for Each Other

Pray for the peace of Jerusalem:
"May those who love you prosper."

PSALM 122:6 GNT

Rachel, Cloe, and Michelle worked in the same department. They had been hired at about the same time and had become fast friends. Unlike Rachel and Cloe, Michelle's spirituality included regular

prayer. She frequently talked with her friends openly about praying. Rachel and Cloe respected this, although this was not something they were accustomed to doing themselves.

Then one day a crisis arose that affected all three of them: Their department was going to be shut down. "I have been praying for you two all along," Michelle said, "but not specifically about this. Let's ask God together to help us through this specific problem."

Rachel said, "I don't think I know how to pray anymore."

"It may be too late," Cloe said.

Michelle took each one by the hand and bowed her head. "Dear God," she began. The women felt their spirits lift almost immediately.

You can bring the welfare and cares of your friends
to God, praying regularly that they may lead
healthy, full, and productive lives.

Let everyone who trusts you be happy; let them sing glad songs forever. Protect those who love you and who are happy because of you. LORD, you bless those who do what is right; you protect them like a soldier's shield.

PSALM 5:11–12 NCV

Friends Walk in Each Other's Shoes

Lord, all my desire is before You;
and my sighing is not hidden from You.

PSALM 38:9 NKJV

erry had a mental picture of Alexis getting ready for the appointment. She would be tense but controlled. She would be focusing her thoughts on a positive outcome and praying for help. On the drive to the clinic, she would be praying and trying to notice things of beauty—like flowers, children, sunshine, and birds. And underneath it all, she would be scared.

Terry was pained that her friend Alexis had to go through this ordeal. Terry had talked to her late last night and again early this morning, reassuring her and consoling her. She made Alexis promise to call her as soon as she returned, even though the results of the biopsy would take a week to come back. Terry would be there for her friend all week long, cheering and encouraging her.

Good friends truly identify with each other and
participate in one another's joys and trials. You feel
what the other feels, as God does for everyone.

If I take the wings of the morning and settle at the farthest limits of the sea, even there your hand shall lead me, and your right hand shall hold me fast. If I say, "Surely the darkness shall cover me, and the light around me become night," even the darkness is not dark to you; the night is as bright as the day, for darkness is as light to you.

PSALM 139:9–12 NRSV

Friends Have High Claims on Your Heart

Guard me as the apple of your eye.
Hide me in the shadow of your wings.

PSALM 17:8 NLT

Paige had been planning her summer trip to Europe for two years. She was going on a tour with a group of other accountants, so she would have plenty of familiar company. She had budgeted and scheduled precisely, and she had saved hundreds of dollars on nonrefundable airline tickets and hotel accommodations.

Then three days before Paige was to leave from Kennedy Airport in New York, her dear friend Cora's mother and father died in a car accident. The family was devastated. Cora had high-school-age sisters still living at home. It was the end of the world for them and Cora; their grief and shock were overwhelming. Without hesitation, Paige canceled her dream trip and raced to Cora's side. Cora would need help with funeral arrangements; she and her younger sisters were in need of tremendous consolation. There was no question in Paige's mind about the right thing to do.

Loving sacrifice is a quintessential aspect of friendship. You can expect it and welcome it.

The Lord is my strength and my shield;
my heart trusted in Him, and I am helped;
therefore my heart greatly rejoices,
and with my song I will praise Him.

Psalm 28:7 NKJV

Friends Survive Tough Tests of the Relationship

In all my years I have never seen the Lord
forsake a man who loves him.

PSALM 37:25 TLB

*N*othing stings like the betrayal of a friend. In his songs, David often referred to the ill treatment he received from friends and relatives when he was down on his luck. His hurt and disappointment were profound. It is sometimes hard to stand by your friends when they are foolish and inconsiderate. And it is hard to work through the bitter disappointment when friends let you down.

Trust is the essence of friendship; once that is broken, it is difficult to mend. People may mean well, but they slip and fall somewhere between intention and execution. This is why God must be your ideal in matters of love and friendship. By keeping him clearly before you, you will far surpass the kind of friend you could be on your own.

You must be ready with the necessary strength and
stamina to overcome the tough tests of friendship.
You can take inspiration from God's example to be
an agent of his love in the world.

You made me; you created me.
Now give me the sense to follow
your commands. May all who fear
you find in me a cause for joy, for
I have put my hope in your word.

PSALM 119:73–74 NLT

Friends Are Allies

Our steps are made firm by the LORD,
when he delights in our way.

PSALM 37:23 NRSV

When Edmund Hillary and his guide, Tenzing, made their historic climb up Mount Everest, they worked hand and glove together to accomplish that feat. Coming down from the peak, Hillary suddenly lost his footing and went into a treacherous slide. Tenzing held taut the line to which he was tied to Hillary and kept them both from falling by digging his ax into the ice.

Later, when interviewed by reporters, Tenzing refused any credit for saving Hillary's life. He considered what he had done a routine part of his job. He put it this way: "Mountain climbers always help each other."

You and your friends have many mountains to climb and will be more successful if you help each other climb them. You have had many helpers. You stand on many shoulders. Much of who you are came from someone else. Wherever you are today, you have had a lot of help in getting there. There is no such thing as a self-made person.

*Y*ou give me a better
way to live, so I live
as you want me to.

PSALM 18:36 NCV

Friends Are Fellow Pilgrims

Give your burdens to the Lord.
He will carry them.

PSALM 55:22 TLB

Your life is a prelude to a greater life to come. You are on your way, with every breath you draw, to full and complete fellowship with God, where all your restlessness and troubles will vanish. You are a pilgrim in the here and now, seeking the face of God. This is the longing that underlies all your strivings. You desperately need and want to walk with God and draw near to him every moment.

Keep this truth foremost in your mind at all times as you go about your earthly business and interact with your friends. Whatever aids and abets your quest for God is good; anything that diverts you from the path is bad and a waste of time. Your friends are fellow pilgrims with you on your journey to God.

As you search about for God, keep your eyes on your goal. Always keep in mind the prize you are reaching for, and encourage your friends to do the same.

Teach me to do thy will; for thou art my God: thy spirit is good; lead me into the land of uprightness. Quicken me, O LORD, for thy name's sake: for thy righteousness' sake bring my soul out of trouble.

PSALM 143:10–11 KJV

Friends Are Soul Mates

He made their hearts and understands
everything they do.

PSALM 33:15 NCV

Terra and Gaye were like sisters. They participated in each other's life and were very much alike. They had grown up together in the same small southern town, where everyone knew them and they knew everyone. Their families worshiped at the same tiny white frame church.

When the time came to go to college, they both went to the state university two hundred miles away and roomed together. Their relationship was based on years of shared memories and an unflinching trust and understanding of each other. Away from the greenhouse environment of their tiny hometown, life started throwing surprising and sometimes frightening challenges at them. They were stretched by these new experiences. And through it all, because of the wonderful blessing of friendship, they had each other.

Thank God for your friends. He will help you to
be the kind of friend who stands by and endures,
the kind of friend who accepts and loves others
for who and what they are.

With my whole heart I have sought You; oh, let me not wander from Your commandments! Your word I have hidden in my heart, that I might not sin against You.

PSALM 119:10–11 NKJV

Friends Care About the Things You Care About

You will show me the way of life.

PSALM 16:11 NLT

*J*eb's new puppy wandered off one afternoon before he got home from school. Jeb went from door to door in the neighborhood, looking for her and putting out the alert that his puppy was loose. Other kids joined in the hunt and fanned out in a half-mile radius from

Jeb's house, checking every possible spot a puppy could hide. Parents who were home telephoned others in the neighborhood, and some even got into their cars and slowly cruised the area, looking for the lost puppy.

After night fell, they called off the search until morning. Disappointed, Jeb dragged himself back home. His mother called to

him when he walked in the door. "Jeb! I found the puppy, honey! She was under the bed!" Jeb went to sleep that night with his puppy and a newfound sense of the loving community surrounding and supporting him.

*Y*ou care about your friends and open your
heart to their concerns and problems. You lend a
hand and offer hope wherever it is needed.

I will extol you, my God and
King, and bless your name
forever and ever. Every day I
will bless you, and praise
your name forever and ever.
Great is the LORD, and
greatly to be praised; his
greatness is unsearchable.

PSALM 145:1–3 NRSV

Friends Share Each Other's Burdens

*I was very worried, but you comforted
me and made me happy.*

PSALM 94:19 NCV

*E*llen's mother was old and infirm. She lived by herself, but Ellen knew the time was coming when her mother wouldn't be able to continue living alone. But her mother was independent and didn't want to burden her family. Even so, Ellen worried about her, and she visited her mother two or three times a day.

Ellen's friends were aware of the stress she was feeling and often accompanied her on her visits. They would take her mother casseroles and tasty desserts and entertaining magazines. It became evident, though, that her mother was in need of more supervision and help. Ellen feared that a terrible accident might happen before Ellen could get to her mother. Ellen's friends came to her rescue. Over several months, they gently persuaded her mother to move in with Ellen by insisting that nothing would make Ellen happier.

*Through your friends, God ministers to you in
marvelous ways. Often, friends are the means by
which God answers your ardent and desperate prayers.*

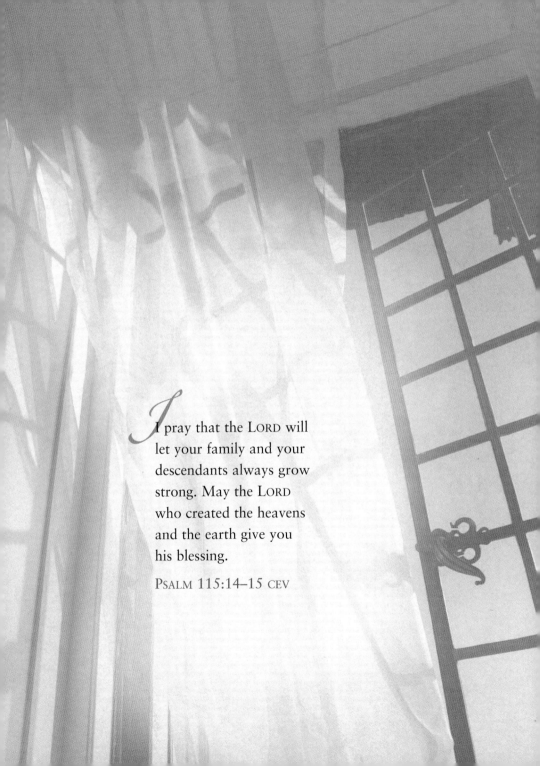

I pray that the LORD will let your family and your descendants always grow strong. May the LORD who created the heavens and the earth give you his blessing.

PSALM 115:14–15 CEV

Friends Love the Things You Love

I am a companion of all who fear You,
and of those who keep Your precepts.

PSALM 119:63 NKJV

Bonnie had a close circle of women friends. They all raised their children together, helping one another along the way, sharing secrets, wishes, and dreams. Eventually their children grew up and were all living independently. Bonnie and her friends were preparing to embark on a new chapter in their lives—new careers, travel, volunteer work, and more.

Then Bonnie came home from her doctor one day with startling news: She was going to have another baby. A host of conflicting feelings crashed over her. She was nearly fifty. She was embarrassed and elated, saddened and overjoyed all at once. Her friends rallied around her and were sympathetic and supportive. She was not in this alone. Her child would be everyone's baby, loved and looked after by all.

You embrace your friends' lives wholly and partake
in the love and devotion your friends have for
others. In so doing, you become part of the family
in God's love and care for the world.

I will tell of your name to my brothers and sisters; in the midst of the congregation I will praise you: You who fear the LORD, praise him! All you offspring of Jacob, glorify him; stand in awe of him, all you offspring of Israel!

PSALM 22:22–23 NRSV

Friends Abide in the Lord

*I entreated Your favor with my whole heart; be
merciful to me according to Your word.*

PSALM 119:58 NKJV

A church setting and the presence of friends sanctify the major events of life. Events such as births, baptisms, weddings, promotions, the acquisition of new homes, and funerals are milestones in life and require an abundance of grace and communal support.

Never miss an opportunity to offer prayer and support to friends when one of these occasions arises. It not only validates and reaffirms your friendship, but is also essential participation in the life of the mystical body of Christ. Blessings flow all around to friends who gather in acknowledgment and celebration of key transitions in an individual friend's life. Your life begins and ends with God; a life well lived abides in him every step of the way. You want the best for yourself and for your friends, and you know that the best can be found only in God.

*Commit yourself to this principle every day, and
rejoice in the special occasions when you can unite
in God's presence to ask his blessing on you.*

Show me the path where I should go, O Lord; point out the right road for me to walk. Lead me; teach me; for you are the God who gives me salvation. I have no hope except in you.

PSALM 25:4–5 TLB

Friends Laugh Together

Oh, give thanks to the LORD, for He is good!
For His mercy endures forever.

PSALM 118:1 NKJV

A college professor had been prepped for surgery and wheeled into the operating room. As he was being transferred from the gurney to

the table, the surgeon made conversation with him to help his patient relax. The surgeon mentioned that he had been a student of the professor's some years before. A smile creased the professor's face. He looked at the table of surgical instruments and then at the doctor. "I hope I passed you," he quipped. Both doctor and patient laughed.

Shared laughter creates bonds of friendship. It is the shortest distance between two people. When people laugh together they cease to be young and old, man and woman, teacher and student. Laughter is what God plants in your soul so you might be refreshed.

When you laugh with your friends you get at least
twice the blessing. And when you and your friends
laugh together, you experience God's grace because
laughter is a reflection of God's love and mercy.
Laughter is God's comment on his creation.

The voice of the LORD echoes from the clouds.
The God of glory thunders through the skies.
So powerful is his voice; so full of majesty.

PSALM 29:3-4 TLB

Friends Share Memories

Return to your rest, O my soul,
for the LORD has dealt bountifully with you.

PSALM 116:7 NKJV

One of the great pleasures of friendship is visiting the treasury of memories built up over time. When you share an experience, good or bad, with a friend, it becomes something valuable and serves to bind

friends closer together. Your lives become established conjointly on a firm foundation, and your allegiance and affection for each other grow stronger.

The words *Remember when* become a familiar and warm prelude to recounting a story of lives shared and the world overcome.

Unstated, perhaps, are the words *You were there for me* and *I was there for you*. And may it always be thus. As you grow older, the memories mount, and the satisfaction you receive from visiting friends increases. These memories are validating evidence of God's grace at work in your life. They are proof in an often seemingly impersonal universe that you exist and that you matter.

Thank God for the wonderful blessings of
your friends. In them you find his love,
purpose, and direction.

From east to west, the
powerful LORD God has
been calling together
everyone on earth.

PSALM 50:1 CEV

Friends Are a Source of Grace for Each Other

He satisfies the longing soul,
and fills the hungry soul with goodness.

PSALM 107:9 NKJV

In a wrenching twist of fate, Emma's husband's business went under in the same month her daughter announced she wanted to marry her longtime boyfriend. Emma had always dreamed of a large church wedding with a lovely reception for her only daughter. Now she had been hit with a double whammy: serious financial consequences for their family as well as no resources to celebrate her daughter's big day.

Emma's friends at church learned of the family's misfortune. Emma had always been extremely generous and giving, and it hurt them to see her in this situation. So they decided to get together and make matters right. Everyone chipped in time and energy to organize a traditional wedding ceremony with a beautiful reception following at the local women's club. Invitations were printed and sent out. A gorgeous dress just the right size was found. The couple took their wedding vows in a church packed with well-wishers and true friends.

Your friends are a favored source for the flow
of God's love and blessings.

The steps of the godly are directed by the LORD.
He delights in every detail of their lives.
Though they stumble, they will not fall,
for the LORD holds them by the hand.

PSALM 37:23–24 NLT

Friends Are a Shield Against Evil

He keeps you from all evil, and preserves your life.

PSALM 121:7 TLB

Tina was short on her tax deposits for the year and worried because she hadn't set the money aside to settle up on April 15. If she had to, she could sell some stock or one of the many fine antiques she had been collecting for nearly twenty years. She was talking this over with Noreen, her tennis buddy, after they finished a set. "Next year should be a good year for the market, and my antiques are irreplaceable. They've taken me a lifetime to acquire."

Noreen nodded somberly. "It's a tough decision," she agreed.

"I was thinking of not reporting some cash transactions so I could come in even and not have to sell anything," Tina said in a whisper. "Who'd be the wiser?"

"You would, Tina," Noreen said grimly. "You and God."

As a friend, you must be capable of tough love. God wants you to care for your friends as much as he does, and that means pointing out when they are in the wrong.

Turn from evil and do good, and you will live in the land forever. For the LORD loves justice, and he will never abandon the godly. He will keep them safe forever, but the children of the wicked will perish.

PSALM 37:27–28 NLT

Friends Are Pleasing in the Eyes of the Lord

Let the favor of the Lord our God be upon us.

PSALM 90:17 NRSV

Friendship is dynamic. It moves, forms, and reforms according to the circumstances and changes of your life. Friendship is an active, lively process in which people unite and ally themselves with others. You involve yourself in the care of others, and you are always there for them. You are ready to answer when they call on you for help and ready and willing to help, even if they don't realize that they want and need your help.

This is how it should be. From the beginning, according to Genesis, God did not intend for people to be alone in this world. Instead, God gave people soulful companions to help handle the strife and toil of life. God bestowed one of the greatest blessings known to humankind—the joy and comfort derived from true friendship.

If you allow him to, God will bless all your friends and the ties that bind you together. He will unite you in his love and teach you to be committed to one another.

He has given me a new song to sing, a hymn of praise to our God. Many will see what he has done and be astounded. They will put their trust in the LORD.

PSALM 40:3 NLT

Notes

SOLDIERS
and
SAILORS

What Do They Do?

By CARLA GREENE — Pictures by LEONARD KESSLER

An I CAN READ Book

HARPER & ROW, PUBLISHERS

New York, Evanston, and London

To Paul Kessler,

my favorite book critic,

with many thanks

for his help.

SOLDIERS AND SAILORS—What Do They Do?
Text copyright © 1963 by Carla Greene,
Pictures copyright © 1963 by Leonard Kessler
Printed in the United States of America.
All Rights Reserved
Library of Congress catalog card number: 63-15325

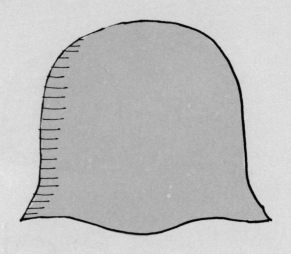

SOLDIERS
and SAILORS

helmet

gas mask

bugle

mess

ABOUT SOLDIERS

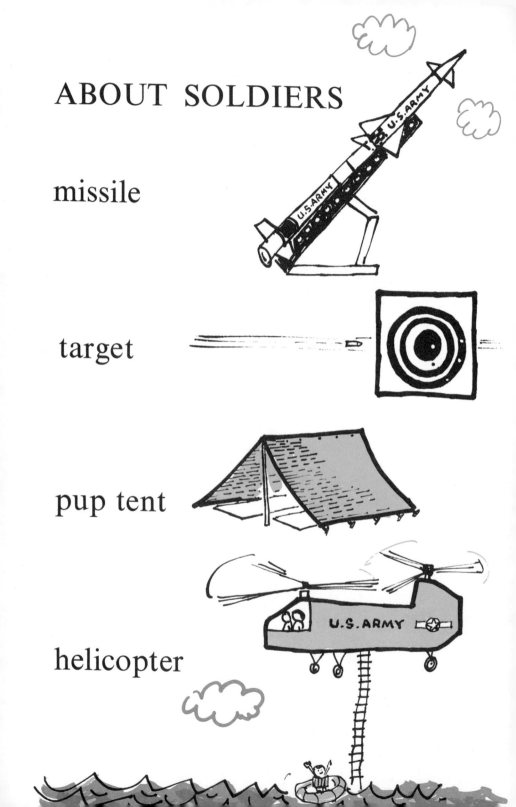

missile

target

pup tent

helicopter

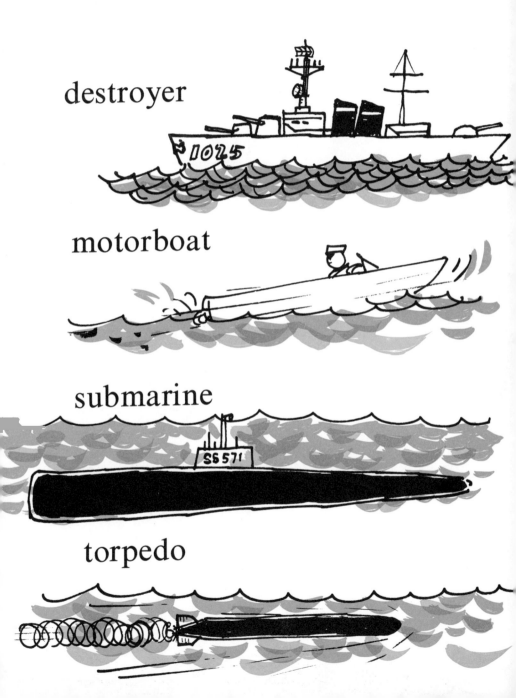

destroyer

motorboat

submarine

torpedo

ABOUT SAILORS

lifeboat

bunk

chow

aircraft carrier

65

The author wishes to thank personnel of the
U.S. Army and U.S. Navy Public Information
Offices at Los Angeles, California, for reading
the manuscript of this book and offering
valuable suggestions.

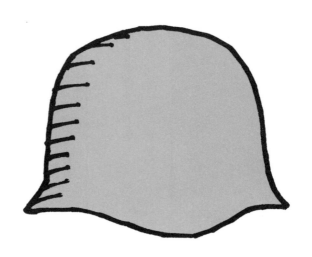

SOLDIERS

Here is Tom, the soldier.

He is in the United States Army.

He is strong. He is brave.

He helps to keep us safe.

Tom wears a tan suit in summer.

He wears a dark-green suit in winter.

He also has a green work suit.

He wears a cap with a badge on it.

He also has a small soft cap,

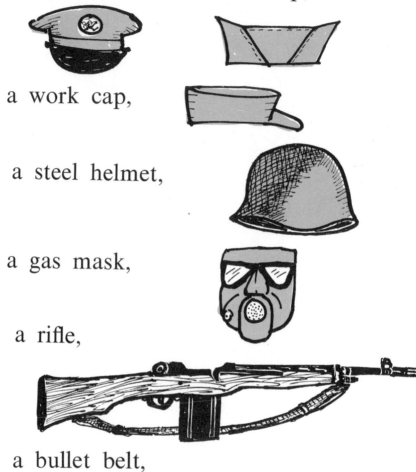

a work cap,

a steel helmet,

a gas mask,

a rifle,

a bullet belt,

and other things he needs.

Tom lives at an Army missile base.

Early in the morning

he hears the bugle call:

Ta-RAH-ra-ra-RAH!

Ta-RAH-ra-ra-RAH!

It is time to get up.

Out of bed, soldiers!

Quick, quick!

Tom gets dressed

and hurries outside.

Up goes the flag.

The soldiers salute the flag.

Then they hurry to roll call.

One by one their names are called.

"Present," says each soldier.

After roll call

the soldiers exercise.

Up, down! Up, down!

Then they make their beds.

16

Now it is time for breakfast.

In the army all meals

are called *mess*.

The soldiers get lots of

good food at morning mess.

The bugle calls again.

It is time for drill.

The soldiers line up.

An officer calls commands:

Right face!

Left face!

Shoulder arms!

Forward march!

Tom and the other soldiers

drill for an hour or two.

Then they go to school.

They learn how to be good soldiers.

19

In the afternoon Tom learns

to do many things.

He learns to shoot at a target.

Bang! Bang! Bang!

At first Tom cannot hit the target.

But he shoots and shoots.

One day Tom hits the center.

BULL'S-EYE!

Now Tom can shoot well.

Next he will learn

to fire the missiles.

One night

Tom goes on guard duty.

Missiles must be kept secret.

Tom has a dog, Hans, to help him.

They must stop anyone who tries

to go in or out of the base.

22

Soldiers do many important jobs.

Tom sends radio messages.

Some soldiers fix the guns.

Some fix the trucks.

Some cook and serve the food.

Some do many other things.

One day there is news!

The soldiers are ready

for battle practice.

They will go on a long march.

Tom puts a pack on his back.

The pack has many things in it:

a blanket,

a raincoat,

a mess kit,

a razor, a toothbrush,

a towel,

and half a pup tent.

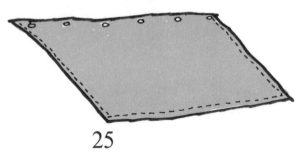

March! March! March!

Many of the soldiers go on foot.

But some ride in big trucks

that look like tanks.

26

Other trucks go along too.

Some trucks carry guns.

One truck has a kitchen in it.

Big tanks follow the trucks.

Planes and helicopters fly over them.

At noon the leader cries "Halt!"

It is time for mess.

The soldiers take out

their mess kits.

They line up at the kitchen truck

and have their plates filled

with good food.

They sit on the ground to eat.

Then after a short rest
the soldiers march on again.
At last they reach the spot
where they will set up camp.

29

Tom puts up his half of a tent.

Another soldier puts up

the half he has been carrying.

They put the two parts together.

Now they have a tent to share.

After evening mess

the soldiers do many things.

They clean their guns.

Some help clean up the kitchen.

Some fix and clean the trucks.

Soon the soldiers get sleepy.

Tom and most of the others

go to their tents to sleep.

But a few soldiers

stand guard for the night.

Everything in the camp

must be kept safe.

The next morning

the soldiers are on the march again.

Soon they come to the place

for their practice battle.

Here comes a big tank.

Boom! Boom! Boom!

The soldiers in the tank

shoot their guns.

The soldiers on the ground

shoot big guns at the tanks.

Of course, it is

a make-believe battle.

The bullets are not real.

But the soldiers learn

what to do if they ever

have to fight a real battle.

When the practice battle ends,

the soldiers march back

to their home camp.

Tom is proud he is a soldier.

Our soldiers always stand ready

to protect our country.

They help to keep us safe.

SAILORS

Here is Jack, the sailor.

He is in the United States Navy.

He is strong. He is brave.

He helps to keep us safe.

In winter Jack wears

a dark-blue suit.

In summer he wears a white suit.

For heavy work he wears

a light-blue work suit.

40

Jack is a new sailor.

He lives at a Navy base.

It is near a big lake.

He learns to row a boat

and to swim well.

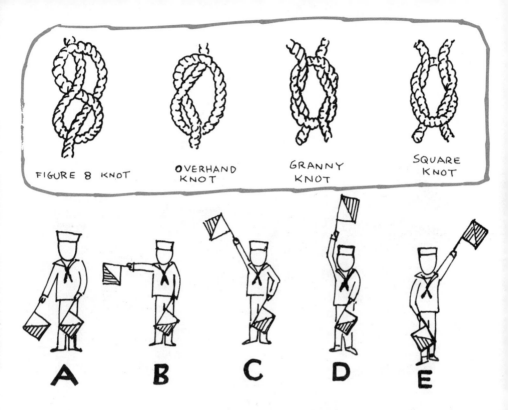

FIGURE 8 KNOT   OVERHAND KNOT   GRANNY KNOT   SQUARE KNOT

A   B   C   D   E

Jack and the other sailors

learn to live at sea.

They learn to obey commands.

They also learn

to tie many kinds of knots,

to signal with flags,

to salute, to march, and to shoot.

42

After a few months

the sailors go to sea.

Some go on small ships

and some go on big ships.

Jack goes to sea on a big ship
with many planes on its deck.
It is called an aircraft carrier.
The planes take off from the deck
and land on it.

Here is Jack

on the aircraft carrier.

Early in the morning

he hears a shrill whistle

and a voice calling:

"Up all hands! Up all hands!"

Jack and the other sailors

jump out of their bunks.

Jack and some other sailors

go up to the deck.

Swish, swash! Swish, swash!

They mop the decks.

Everything on a ship must shine.

Soon it is time for morning *chow*.

All meals in the Navy

are called chow.

The sailors get plenty to eat.

After chow the sailors

line up on deck for roll call.

Jack hears his name.

He says, "Present."

Now the sailors go off

to do many kinds of jobs.

Some sailors

clean and fix the planes.

Some help to steer the ship.

Some help the engineer

to keep the boilers hot.

Some are cooks and bakers.

Some do other important things.

Sailors have many kinds

of drills aboard ship.

A bell goes *Clang! Clang! Clang!*

It is a fire drill.

Quick, quick, sailors!

Each man to his place.

Roll out the hose.

Put out the make-believe fire!

51

Sometimes when the bell clangs

it is for a lifeboat drill.

Into the lifeboats

go Jack and the other sailors.

Lower the boats! *Row, row, row!*

At last a big day comes.

It is time to practice

sending off the planes.

The deck is too short

for the big jet planes

to take off without help.

So the sailors must help

to get the planes into the air.

53

Jack and some other sailors

push a big jet plane

in front of a machine.

The machine works like a slingshot.

Other sailors pull a lever

and the plane goes shooting

into the sky.

R-r-roar! R-r-roar!

Flames and smoke

shoot from the engines.

Zoom! Zoom! Zoom!

One after the other

the jets take off.

The jets shoot off their guns.

They drop bombs.

They fire missiles.

Rat-a-tat-tat! go the guns.

Boom! Boom! go the bombs.

Swish! Swish! Swish!

go the missiles.

A helicopter follows the planes.

A small ship called a destroyer

follows the planes too.

Once in a while something goes wrong
with a plane's engine.

Splash! The plane falls into the sea.

Off goes the helicopter to save the pilot.

Sailors on the destroyer

jump into a motorboat.

They go to help the pilot too.

The helicopter drops a hook

to the pilot.

But the waves are too big.

The pilot cannot reach the hook.

Then the sailors in the motorboat

pull the pilot into their boat.

The pilot is saved!

Some sailors go to sea

on a submarine.

Down, down, they go!

They live under the water

for weeks or months.

Sometimes the aircraft carrier

and the destroyer

chase the submarine.

They make believe

it is an enemy submarine.

There is a machine on the destroyer

that picks up sounds

in the water.

A sailor listens to the sounds.

He can tell where the submarine is.

He signals the aircraft carrier.

Planes take off from the carrier.

Boom! Boom! Boom!

The planes drop bombs

that explode under the water.

The destroyer fires torpedoes.

The submarine dives down, down!

It gets away from the attack.

Soon the submarine chase is over.

All the sailors go back

to their other duties.

Jack is proud he is a sailor.

Our sailors, our ships,

and our planes

always stand ready

to protect our country.

They help to keep us safe.

HIGHLANDS ELEMENTARY SCHOOL
LIBRARY MEDIA CENTER
2022 Colonist Park
Sugar Land, Texas 77478

355.3 Greene, Carla 1306
GRE
       Soldiers and sailors

DATE